# DINOSAUR PROFILES

# SCIPIONYX

Published in 2004 in North America by Blackbirch Press. Blackbirch Press is an imprint of Thomson Gale, a part of the Thomson Corporation.

Thomson is a trademark and Gale [and Blackbirch Press] are registered trademarks used herein under license.

*For more information, contact*
The Gale Group, Inc.
27500 Drake Rd.
Farmington Hills, MI 48331-3535
Or you can visit our Internet site at http://www.gale.com

Computer illustrations 3D and 2D: Leonello Calvetti and Luca Massini

Photographs: pages 22, 23 M. Bianchi/Farabolafoto

The drawings of bones and skeleton of Scipionyx are based on original reconstructions by Marco Auditore

LIBRARY OF CONGRESS CATALOGING-IN-PUBLICATION DATA

Dalla Vecchia, Fabio Marco.
  Scipionyx / text by Fabio Marco Dalla Vecchia; illustrations by Leonello Calvetti and Luca Massini.
    p. cm. — (Dinosaurs profiles)
  Includes bibliographical references and index.
  ISBN 1-4103-0496-5 (paperback : alk. paper)
  ISBN 1-4103-0334-9 (hardback : alk. paper)
   1. Scipionyx—Juvenile literature. I. Calvetti, Leonello. II. Massini, Luca. III. Title. IV. Series: Dalla Vecchia, Fabio Marco. Dinosaur profiles.

  QE862.S3D42 2004
  567.912—dc22                                                           2004008698

Printed in China
10 9 8 7 6 5 4 3 2 1

# CONTENTS

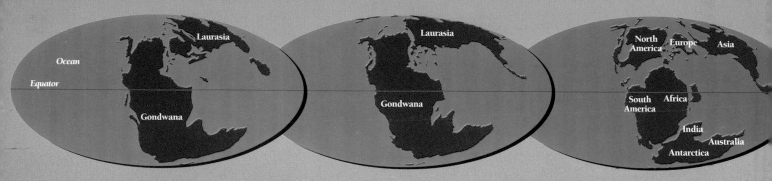

| Late Triassic | Early Jurassic | Middle Jurassic |
|---|---|---|
| 227–206 million years ago | 206–176 million years ago | 176–159 million years ago |

# A CHANGING WORLD

Earth's long history began 4.6 billion years ago. Dinosaurs are some of the most fascinating animals from the planet's long past.

The word *dinosaur* comes from the word *dinosauria*. This word was invented by the English scientist Richard Owen in 1842. It comes from two Greek words, *deinos* and *sauros*. Together, these words mean "terrifying lizards."

The dinosaur era, also called the Mesozoic era, lasted from 248 million years ago to 65 million years ago. It is divided into three periods. The first, the Triassic period, lasted 42 million years. The second, the Jurassic period, lasted 61 million years. The third, the Cretaceous period, lasted 79 million years. Dinosaurs ruled the world for a huge time span of 160 million years.

Like dinosaurs, mammals appeared at the end of the Triassic period. During the time of dinosaurs, mammals were small animals the size of a mouse. Only after dinosaurs became extinct did mammals develop into the many forms that exist today. Humans never met Mesozoic dinosaurs. The dinosaurs

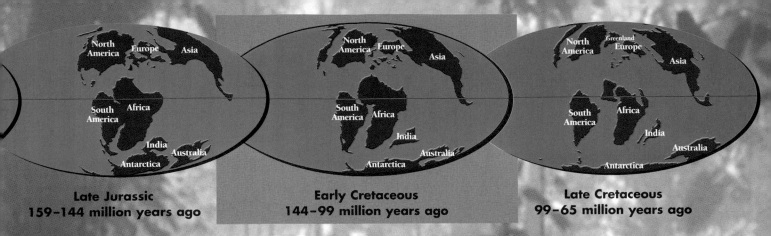

**Late Jurassic**
159–144 million years ago

**Early Cretaceous**
144–99 million years ago

**Late Cretaceous**
99–65 million years ago

were gone nearly 65 million years before humans appeared on Earth.

Dinosaurs changed in time. *Stegosaurus* and *Brachiosaurus* no longer existed when *Tyrannosaurus* and *Triceratops* appeared 75 million years later.

The dinosaur world was different from today's world. The climate was warmer, with few extremes. The position of the continents was different. Plants were constantly changing, and grass did not even exist.

7

# A Small Dinosaur

The only *Scipionyx* found to date is a young one. It was probably just a little older than a hatchling when it died. Scientists have nicknamed the little dinosaur Skippy. The fossil is about 15 to 18 inches (40 to 45 cm) long and 4 to 5 inches (10 to 12 cm) tall. It weighs only 1 pound (500 g). Its head is a little more than 2 inches (5 cm) long, and is large compared to the rest of the body.

*Scipionyx* lived during the Cretaceous period about 110 million years ago. It lived on an island in the middle of the Tethys Ocean, between Africa and Eurasia. The geography of the area has changed since then. Today, all that is left of the Tethys Ocean is the Mediterranean Sea. The islands in it were squeezed together when Africa collided with Europe. They became the mountains of southern Europe. *Scipionyx* was found in one of those mountains in the Apennines of southern Italy.

*Scipionyx* might have been a dwarf species. Paleontologists think an adult was no more than about 5 feet (1.5 m) long and weighed only 55 to 66 pounds (25 to 30 kg). It was very small compared to the large carnivorous dinosaurs that lived in North America at the time. Animals that live on islands are usually smaller than species that live on continents. This is probably because there is usually less food available on islands.

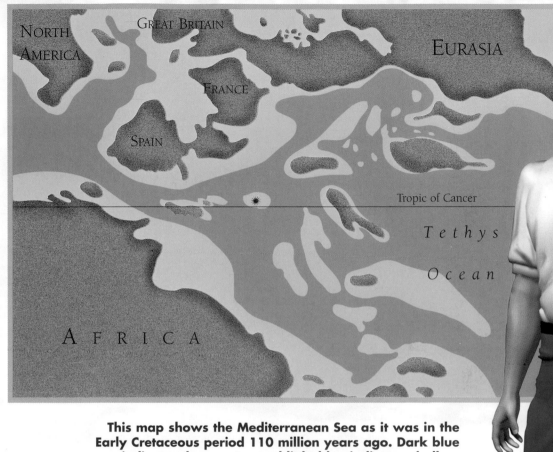

**This map shows the Mediterranean Sea as it was in the Early Cretaceous period 110 million years ago. Dark blue indicates deep water and light blue indicates shallow water. The red spot marks the only place where a *Scipionyx* fossil has been found.**

# SCIPIONYX BABIES

A *Scipionyx* mother laid its eggs in the sand on the coast of a flat tropical island. The white, soft sand was made of tiny pieces of shells. The mother was too large to sit on the eggs as birds do. There were few predators on the island, but the mother probably kept watch over the eggs and hatchlings.

# SEARCHING FOR FOOD

Shortly after birth, a *Scipionyx* hatchling was already able to provide food for itself. As a predator, it had an instinct to hunt. Despite its young age, it had about fifty sharp, pointed teeth that already worked. Two teeth in the upper jaw were longer than the others. They were used to hold down wriggling prey. The front legs were long and ended with large hands. *Scipionyx* used its curved claws to grasp its prey.

*Scipionyx* hatchlings were more curious and intelligent than many other dinosaurs. The surrounding world was new to them, however. They needed to explore it carefully.

# After the Storm

Sometimes, violent tropical storms struck the islands. Many dead fish and shrimp were stranded on the beach. After a storm, the lagoon became stagnant. This made the water poisonous to marine animals. It had too much algae and not enough oxygen. Those animals that did not escape to the open sea had no chance to survive. They died and fell to the bottom of the sea or were stranded on the beach. This left a lot of food for *Scipionyx*.

# Danger on the Shore

A tidal flat is a flat zone between the sea and the land. It is exposed and then covered up by the tides. Waves carry the bodies of floating dead animals to the shore. During low tide, predators and scavengers would run across the flats looking for something to eat. *Scipionyx* also looked for food there, but it had to be careful. There could be dangerous large animals such as crocodiles on the shore.

# THE SCIPIONYX BODY

The *Scipionyx* skeleton is missing most of the tail and the back legs. They were lost when the slab containing the fossil was broken. There is a small wishbone, like a bird's, in the chest. The *Scipionyx* fossil contains body parts that usually do not fossilize. It has intestines, muscles, and part of the liver and trachea (windpipe). In fossils, these organs are usually completely destroyed by decay or eaten by scavengers.

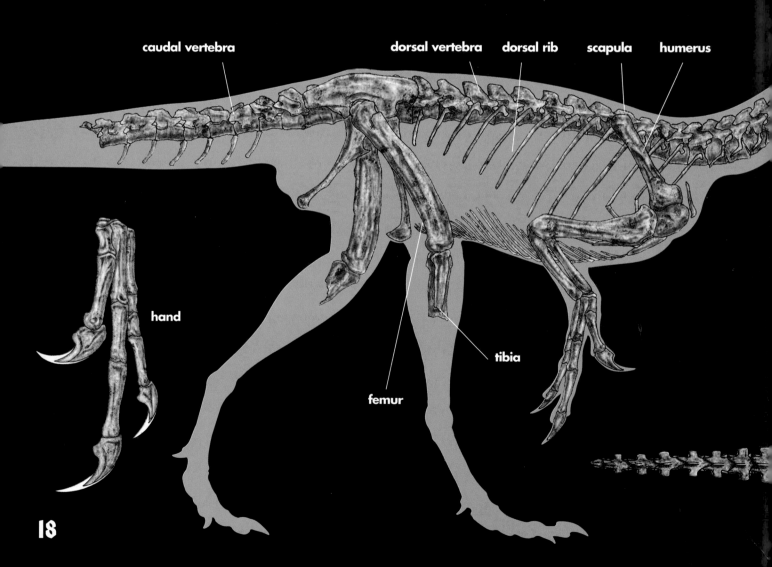

caudal vertebra — dorsal vertebra — dorsal rib — scapula — humerus — hand — femur — tibia

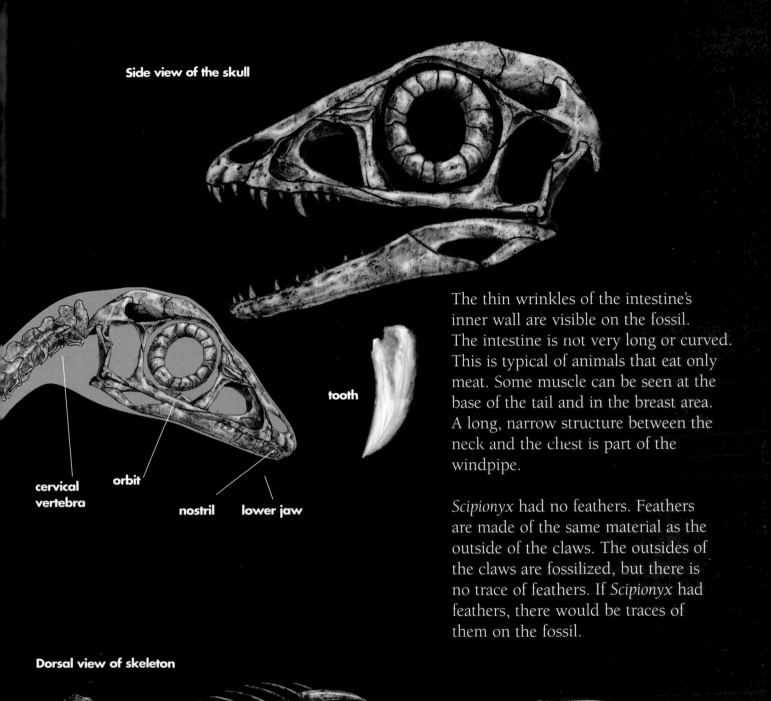

**Side view of the skull**

cervical vertebra

orbit

nostril

lower jaw

tooth

**Dorsal view of skeleton**

The thin wrinkles of the intestine's inner wall are visible on the fossil. The intestine is not very long or curved. This is typical of animals that eat only meat. Some muscle can be seen at the base of the tail and in the breast area. A long, narrow structure between the neck and the chest is part of the windpipe.

*Scipionyx* had no feathers. Feathers are made of the same material as the outside of the claws. The outsides of the claws are fossilized, but there is no trace of feathers. If *Scipionyx* had feathers, there would be traces of them on the fossil.

# Digging Up Scipionyx

*Scipionyx* is unique, so it is very valuable. The skeleton was discovered in 1981 by Giovanni Tedesco, a fossil collector from northern Italy. He found the fossil in the white limestone near the small town of Pietraroja, in the middle of the Apennine Mountains of southern Italy. Several fossils of fish and other marine animals had been found there in the past. Tedesco did not realize that he had found a small dinosaur. He thought it was a bird with teeth, so he nicknamed it "the little dog" because of the teeth.

In 1992, after he saw the dinosaur movie *Jurassic Park*, Tedesco showed the fossil to a paleontologist, who correctly identified it as a small dinosaur. In 1993, the fossil was donated to the Italian government. Paleontologists Cristiano Dal Sasso and Marco Signore named it *Scipionyx* after Italian geologist Scipione Breislak in 1998. *Scipionyx* means "claw of Scipione" in Latin and Greek words.

*Scipionyx's* skeleton does not show any signs of injuries or a violent death. It might have drowned in the sea and immediately sunk to the bottom. There, it was covered by the white mud typical of tropical islands. It became fossilized as the mud became limestone rock. A lucky strike of a hammer split the rock to reveal the skeleton.

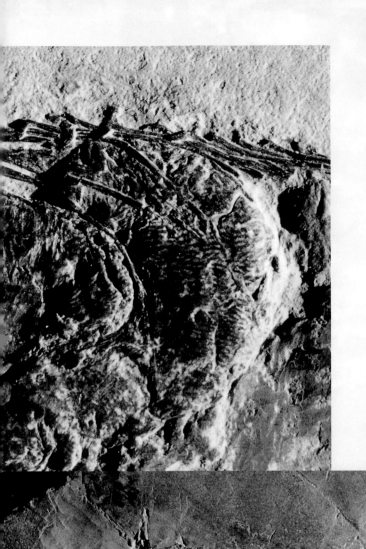

Left: The only *Scipionyx* fossil has some partially preserved internal organs.

Below: The *Scipionyx* fossil was preserved in limestone.

Many scientists believe that the Chicxulub crater off the coast of Mexico was made by a meteorite that led to the extinction of the dinosaurs.

- *Coelurus*, USA, 144–137 million years ago

Places where *Scipionyx, Coelurus,* and *Ornitholestes* fossils have been found are noted on the map.

*Scipionyx* is a saurischian theropod. It belongs to a family of small dinosaurs with only one member: *Scipionyx samniticus*. It is different from other theropods because it evolved on an island, far away from continents. *Scipionyx* is not closely related to any other dinosaurs. Its closest relatives may be *Coelurus* and *Ornitholestes*.

# SCIPIONYX RELATIVES

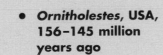

- **Ornitholestes, USA, 156–145 million years ago**

- **Scipionyx, Italy, ca. 110 million years ago**

# THE GREAT EXTINCTION

Sixty-five million years ago, about 50 million years after the time of *Scipionyx,* dinosaurs became extinct. This may have happened because a large meteorite struck Earth. A wide crater caused by a meteorite exactly 65 million years ago has been located along the coast of the Yucatán Peninsula in Mexico. The impact of the meteorite would have produced an enormous amount of dust. This dust would have stayed suspended in the atmosphere and blocked sunlight for a long time. A lack of sunlight would have caused a drastic drop of the earth's temperature and killed plants. The plant-eating dinosaurs would have died, starved and frozen. As a result, meat-eating dinosaurs would have had no prey and would also have starved.

Some scientists believe dinosaurs did not die out completely. They think that birds were feathered dinosaurs that survived the great extinction. That would make the present-day chicken and all of its feathered relatives descendants of the large dinosaurs.

# THE EVOLUTION OF DINOSAURS

The oldest dinosaur fossils are 220–225 million years old and have been found mainly in South America. They have also been found in Africa, India, and North America. Dinosaurs probably evolved from small and nimble bipedal reptiles like the Triassic *Lagosuchus* of Argentina. Dinosaurs were able to rule the world because their legs were held directly under the body, like those of modern mammals. This made them faster and less clumsy than other reptiles.

Since 1887, dinosaurs have been divided into two groups based on the structure of their hips. Saurischian dinosaurs had hips shaped like those of modern lizards. Ornithischian dinosaurs had hips shaped like those of modern birds.

**Triceratops is one of the Ornithischian dinosaurs, whose hip bones (inset) are shaped like those of modern birds.**

Tyrannosaurus is in the Saurischian group of dinosaurs, whose hip bones (inset) are shaped like those of modern lizards.

There are two main groups of saurischians. One group is sauropodomorphs. This group includes sauropods, such as *Brachiosaurus*. Sauropods ate plants and were quadrupedal, meaning they walked on four legs. The other group of saurischians, theropods, includes bipedal meat-eating predators. Some paleontologists believe birds are a branch of theropod dinosaurs.

Ornithischians are all plant eaters. They are divided into three groups. Thyreophorans include the quadrupedal stegosaurians, including *Stegosaurus*, and ankylosaurians, including *Ankylosaurus*. The other two groups are ornithopods, which includes *Edmontosaurus* and marginocephalians.

# A Dinosaur's Family Tree

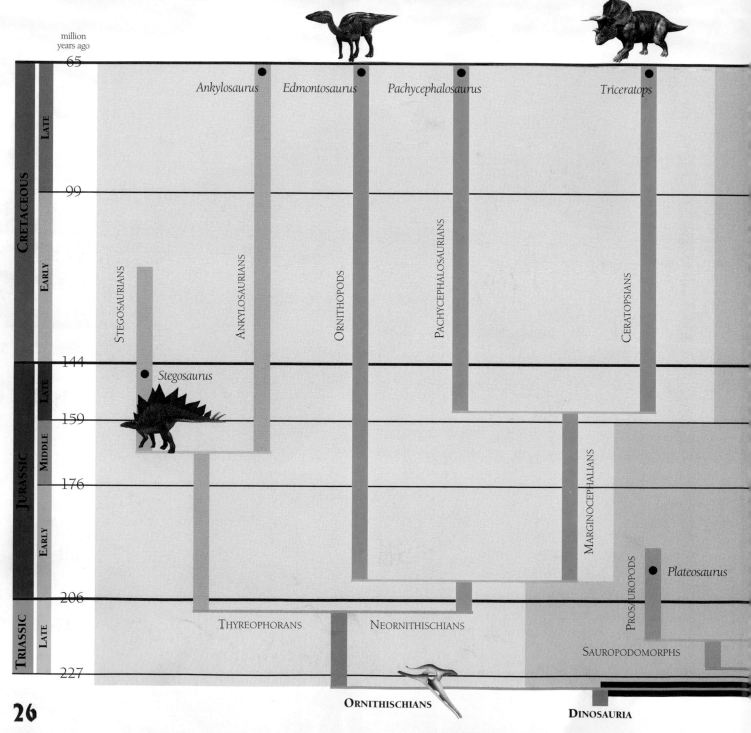

million years ago

CRETACEOUS
JURASSIC
TRIASSIC

LATE
EARLY
LATE
MIDDLE
EARLY
LATE

65
99
144
159
176
206
227

Ankylosaurus
Edmontosaurus
Pachycephalosaurus
Triceratops

STEGOSAURIANS
ANKYLOSAURIANS
ORNITHOPODS
PACHYCEPHALOSAURIANS
CERATOPSIANS
MARGINOCEPHALIANS
PROSAUROPODS

Stegosaurus
Plateosaurus

THYREOPHORANS
NEORNITHISCHIANS
SAUROPODOMORPHS

ORNITHISCHIANS
DINOSAURIA

Ornithomimus

Tyrannosaurus

ORNITHOMIMOIDEANS

TYRANNOSAUROIDS

OVIRAPTOROSAURIANS

DEINONYCHOSAURIANS

BIRDS

Scipionyx

Deinonychus

SAUROPODS

Caudipteryx

Brachiosaurus

ORNITHOLESTES

THEROPODS

SAURISCHIANS

27

# Glossary

**Bipedal**  moving on two feet

**Bone**  hard tissue made mainly of calcium phosphate

**Caudal**  related to the tail

**Cervical**  related to the neck

**Claws**  sharp, pointed nails on the fingers and toes of predators

**Cretaceous Period**  the period of geological time between 144 and 65 million years ago

**Dorsal**  related to the back

**Egg**  a large cell enclosed in a shell produced by reptiles and birds to reproduce themselves

**Feathers**  outgrowth of the skin of birds and some dinosaurs, used in flight and in providing insulation and protection of the body

**Femur**  thigh bone

**Fossil**  a part of an organism of an earlier geologic age, such as a skeleton or leaf imprint, that has been preserved in the earth's crust

**Jurassic Period**  the period of geological time between 206 and 144 million years ago

**Mesozoic Era**  the period of geological time between 248 and 65 million years ago

**Meteorite**  a piece of iron or rock that falls to Earth from space

**Orbit**  the opening in the skull surrounding the eye

**Paleontologist**  a scientist who studies prehistoric life

**Quadrupedal**  moving on four feet

**Scapula**  shoulder blade

**Scavenger**  animal that eats dead animals or plants

**Skeleton**  the structure of an animal body, made up of bones

**Skull**  the bones that form the cranium and the face

**Tibia**  the shinbone

**Triassic Period**  the period of geological time between 248 and 206 million years ago

**Vertebrae**  the bones of the backbone

# FOR MORE INFORMATION

## Books

Paul M. Barrett, *National Geographic Dinosaurs*. Washington, DC: National Geographic Society, 2001.

Tim Haines, *Walking with Dinosaurs: A Natural History*. New York: Dorling Kindersley, 2000.

David Lambert, Darren Naish, and Elizabeth Wyse, *Dinosaur Encyclopedia: From Dinosaurs to the Dawn of Man*. New York: Dorling Kindersley, 2001.

## Web Sites

**The Cyberspace Museum of Natural History**
www.cyberspacemuseum.com/dinohall.html
An online dinosaur museum that includes descriptions and illustrations.

**Dinodata**
www.dinodata.net
A site that includes detailed descriptions of fossils, illustrations, and news about dinosaur research and recent discoveries.

**The Smithsonian National Museum of Natural History**
www.nmnh.si.edu/paleo/dino
A virtual tour of the Smithsonian's National Museum of Natural History dinosaur exhibits.

# ABOUT THE AUTHOR

Fabio Marco Dalla Vecchia is the curator of the Paleontological Museum of Monfalcone in Gorizia, Italy. He has participated in several paleontological field works in Italy and other countries and has directed paleontological excavations in Italy. He is the author of more than fifty scientific articles that have been published in national and international journals.

# INDEX

# INDEX